WEATHER MATH

Math and My World

Kieran Walsh

Rourke
Publishing LLC
Vero Beach, Florida 32964

www.rourkepublishing.com

PHOTO CREDITS:
Cover photo by Corbis.com. All other photos from AbleStock.com, except for page 10 by the author; illustration of men with umbrellas © Getty Images

Technical Advisor: Mike Bono, Chief Meteorologist, Capital News 9, WEAN, Albany, New York

Editor: Frank Sloan

Cover and Interior design by Nicola Stratford
Page layout by Heather Scarborough

Library of Congress Cataloging-in-Publication Data

Walsh, Kieran.
  Weather math / by Kieran Walsh.
      p. cm. -- (Math and my world)
Includes bibliographical references and index.
Contents: The atmosphere -- Temperature -- Wind chill -- Heat index -- Climate, part 1: average annual temperature -- Climate, part 2: precipitation -- Snowfall -- Wind -- Hurricanes and tornadoes.
  ISBN 1-58952-384-9 (hardcover)
  1. Mathematics--Study and teaching (Elementary)--Juvenile literature.
2. Weather--Juvenile literature. 3. Climate--Juvenile literature. [1. Mathematics. 2. Weather. 3. Climate.] I. Title.
  QA135.6.W35 2003
  551.6'01'51--dc22

                                    2003011564

Printed in the USA

w/w

TABLE OF CONTENTS

Introduction 4

The Atmosphere .6

Temperature 10

Climate, Part 1:
Average Annual Temperature 15

Climate, Part 2: Precipitation 22

Snowfall 29

Wind 32

Hurricanes and Tornadoes 37

Conclusion 43

The Metric System 44

Glossary 46

Further Reading .47

Websites to Visit .47

Index 48

INTRODUCTION

Have you ever watched the news on television? If so, you have probably seen the "weather man" give his or her report.

"Weather man" is just a nickname, though. To start with, they can be either men or women! In fact, the correct term for these people is **meteorologist.**

If you have ever listened to your local meteorologists carefully, you've probably heard them refer to lots of numbers to describe amounts of rain or snow, the intensity of an approaching storm, and, of course, the temperature.

And, where there are numbers, there is math!

Believe it or not, a meteorologist has to use math every day to determine what all those numbers mean. After you've read this book, you'll understand what they mean, too!

The earth's troposphere reaches up about 6 miles into the air. Hot air balloons are capable of going slightly higher than that, placing them in the stratosphere, the second layer of the atmosphere. ▶

THE ATMOSPHERE

The definition of a meteorologist is a scientist who studies the behavior of a planet's **atmosphere.** An atmosphere is a layer of gases that surrounds a planet.

There are actually several layers to the earth's atmosphere, but the lowest layer, the one that contains all the gases we depend on to live, is called the **troposphere**.

Like everything to do with weather, the height of the troposphere is always changing. But, generally speaking, the average height of the troposphere around the world is 6 miles. Do you know how many feet that is?

There are 5,280 feet in one mile. To find out how many feet there are in 6 miles, you need to multiply:

$$5280 \times 6 = 31680$$

So you can also say that the troposphere reaches up about 31,680 feet into the air. That's pretty high up! On the other hand, though, the highest mountain in the world, Mount Everest, reaches up 29,028 feet.

What meteorologists refer to as "weather," including the temperature, rainfall, and storms, is all a result of having an atmosphere. It is within the troposphere that all weather takes place!

People who participate in high-altitude sports like this rock climber have to be especially careful because, at great heights, the atmosphere gets "thinner," meaning the oxygen content lessens.

It is also within the troposphere that you can find clouds. Clouds are actually made of millions of little drops of water. Most of the time, the water in the air is in a **vapor**, or gas, state. Clouds form when there is so much water in the atmosphere that it **condenses**, or changes from vapor to liquid.

There are three basic types of clouds: cirrus, cumulus, and stratus. The cloud type you are probably most familiar with are cumulus clouds. Cumulus clouds are big, puffy clouds. Stratus clouds, on the other hand, are layered and flat. Finally, cirrus clouds are thin, wispy clouds.

Along with the three basic types of clouds, there are also clouds that are combinations of different types of clouds. Cirrostratus clouds, for instance, are combinations of cirrus and stratus clouds.

You already know that clouds can be found in the air, but each type of cloud exists at a different **altitude**. Here are some cloud types along with the heights at which they can be found:

Cirrus: 20,000-40,000 feet
Cirrostratus: 20,000-40,000 feet
Cirrocumulus: 20,000-40,000 feet

Altostratus: 6,000-20,000 feet
Altocumulus: 6,000-20,000 feet

Stratocumulus: below 6,000 feet
Stratus: below 6,000 feet
Cumulus: below 6,000 feet
Cumulonimbus: cloud mass from below 6,000 feet to
    over 50,000 feet

Using this data, can you calculate how much higher up a cirrus cloud is compared with a stratus cloud?

Because they are big and puffy, the clouds pictured here are most likely cumulus clouds. Knowing that, how high up would you say these clouds are located?

A cirrus cloud can be anywhere between 20,000 and 40,000 feet. Just to keep things simple, use the lower number: 20,000. Meanwhile, a stratus cloud is typically below 6,000 feet. All you have to do to compare these numbers is to subtract the smaller number from the larger one:

$$20,000 - 6,000 = 14,000$$

So a cirrus cloud is at least 14,000 feet higher up than a stratus cloud!

TEMPERATURE

When people talk about the weather, the outside temperature is usually the first thing they discuss. Perhaps this is because the temperature is something that is constantly changing.

Let's take a look at some temperatures:

103°
65°
-12°

You've probably noticed the little "°" to the right of each of the numbers. That symbol stands for "degrees." And, in addition, you're also talking about *specific types* of degrees. In the United States, we use the Fahrenheit temperature scale.

A familiar sight around any home is a thermometer. A thermometer like this one, which has both a Fahrenheit and Celsius scale, can be a big help when learning how to convert from one scale to the other. Meanwhile, the circular gauge is for measuring humidity.

So, each of these temperatures could also be read as:

103 *degrees Fahrenheit*

65 *degrees Fahrenheit*

-12 *degrees Fahrenheit*

In America, though, it's taken for granted that the degrees being referred to are Fahrenheit. That is why people usually drop the term Fahrenheit and simply say "degrees":

103 *degrees*

65 *degrees*

-12 *degrees*

Meanwhile, you may be wondering about the "-" symbol in front of the last temperature. Does that symbol look familiar to you? It should, because it's a *minus* sign—the same symbol used in subtraction problems. The way you should read that temperature is *minus* 12 degrees.

A glacier is a huge mound of ice. Most glaciers form over a land mass, but sometimes chunks of the ice break off and float into the sea. About what temperature would you say it has to be for glaciers to form?

Water is a key element in temperature scales. For instance, two key points of the Fahrenheit scale are the temperature at which water *freezes*, and the temperature at which water *boils:*

32° = freezing point

212° = boiling point

How many degrees are there between these two numbers?

You can find out by subtracting:

$$212 - 32 = 180$$

There are 180° between the boiling and freezing points on the Fahrenheit temperature scale!

The freezing temperature and the boiling temperature are good reference points to keep in mind. You can use them to figure out what a current temperature means to us. Another reference number you can use is room temperature, the temperature most people feel comfortable with in their homes. Room temperature is around 72°.

Now that you know the numbers for freezing, boiling, and room temperature, review your sample temperatures.

You can probably tell already that 103° is a hot temperature. But how hot is it?

Compare it with room temperature by subtracting the smaller number from the larger one:

$$103 - 72 = 31$$

Wow. 103° is 31 degrees *above* room temperature. That kind of temperature isn't just hot, it's dangerously hot. The best thing to do on a day like that would be to stay indoors and drink plenty of water.

Room temperature, or the temperature at which most people feel comfortable indoors, is around 72°.

Look at the second temperature, 65°. The easiest comparison you can make here is with room temperature. Again, just subtract the smaller number from the larger one:

$$72 - 65 = 7$$

So, 65° is seven degrees lower than room temperature.

65°, then, is comfortable, maybe even a little cool. This is the kind of mild, pleasant day you would experience in the early spring.

Now for the last temperature, minus 12 degrees. The first thing to understand about this temperature is that it is below zero. That is why it is minus 12 degrees—because it is 12 degrees less than zero.

Obviously, this means that a temperature of minus 12 degrees is also below freezing (32 degrees). The question is, how many degrees below freezing is it?

In order to find out, you'll have to use both subtraction and addition. First of all, subtract zero from 32:

$$32 - 0 = 32$$

Next, add the number of degrees below zero the temperature is to 32:

$$32 + 12 = 44$$

Now you know that a temperature of minus 12 degrees is 44 degrees below zero! That's a cold day!

Gabriel Daniel Fahrenheit

A German physicist named Gabriel Daniel Fahrenheit developed the Fahrenheit scale in 1724. Fahrenheit was a creator of scientific instruments. He invented both the alcohol thermometer and the **mercury** thermometer. Mercury is still the standard solution used in most thermometers today.

CLIMATE, PART 1: AVERAGE ANNUAL TEMPERATURE

You already know that weather is constantly changing. However, there are certain patterns that the weather seems to follow in specific locations. For instance, Florida is known as a generally hot, sunny state while North Dakota is thought of as a cold, snowy place.

What we're talking about here is **climate**, the type of weather usually experienced in a particular place over a long period of time. Climate is measured according to two conditions: temperature and **precipitation**.

Hawaii is known as a warm, sunny place. This is a description of Hawaii's climate.

Let's look at the temperature data collected at some prominent weather observing stations in the United States. The first chart lists the places with the ten "warmest" temperatures. As you learned earlier, these numbers are in degrees Fahrenheit:

City	State	Average Annual Temperature
Honolulu	Hawaii	76.975°
Miami	Florida	75.7°
Vero Beach	Florida	72.475°
Tampa	Florida	71.95°
Phoenix	Arizona	71.525°
San Antonio	Texas	68.7°
Houston	Texas	68.225°
Tucson	Arizona	68.15°
New Orleans	Louisiana	68.1°
Austin	Texas	68.075°

*Source: Infoplease.com - Climate of 100 Selected U.S. Cities

Look carefully at the top of the third column. You'll notice it's labeled "Average Annual Temperature." What does that mean?

Let's say that tomorrow you were going to Honolulu, Hawaii. Just because the Average Annual Temperature there is roughly 77° doesn't mean that that's what the temperature will be when you are there. It might be hotter, or it might be colder.

Rather, an average is a number that represents a group of numbers. Believe it or not, you already have a lot of experience with averages. Your grades, for instance, are averages.

How does your teacher calculate your grades? One of the most important factors are your test scores.

Let's say that, during a grading period, you took three tests, and your scores for them were:

$$79$$
$$94$$
$$82$$

Based on these scores, what would your final grade be?

You can find out by calculating the average of the test scores. First of all, add them up:

$$79 + 94 + 82 = 255$$

The next step is to divide the result (255) by the number of **addends**. The addends are the numbers you added together. In this case, there were three addends, 79, 94, and 82:

$$255 \div 3 = 85$$

The average of all your test scores is 85. That means that your average grade is a B!

Average Annual Temperature is calculated in the same way. With temperature, of course, we're dealing with *lots* of numbers. Temperatures are taken not only every day of the year, but at different times of each day. However, you can narrow things down a bit by looking at just four numbers. In this case, consider the temperatures in Honolulu for January, April, July, and October. You've probably noticed that these months roughly coincide with the four seasons—winter, spring, summer, and fall:

January	April	July	October
72.6	75.7	80.1	79.5

*Source: Infoplease.com - Climate of 100 Selected U.S. Cities

Using these temperatures, you can determine the annual average temperature for Honolulu. The first step is to add them up:

$$72.6 + 75.7 + 80.1 + 79.5 = 307.9$$

Then divide the result by the number of addends, which is four:

$$307.9 \div 4 = 76.975$$

And that's how you get the answer of 76.975°—the average annual temperature for Honolulu, Hawaii!

Just for comparison, take a look at the ten "coldest" average temperatures:

City	State	Average Annual Temperature
Burlington	Vermont	44.2°
Helena	Montana	43.35°
Bismarck	North Dakota	41.425°
Fargo	North Dakota	40.825°
Juneau	Alaska	39.6°
Caribou	Maine	39.05°
Duluth	Minnesota	38.55°
Anchorage	Alaska	35.275°
Mt. Washington	New Hampshire	26.675°
Fairbanks	Alaska	26.025°

*Source: Infoplease.com - Climate of 100 Selected U.S. Cities

You already know that the hottest city in the United States is Honolulu, Hawaii, with an average annual temperature of 76.975°. Meanwhile, the coldest city in the United States is Fairbanks, Alaska, with an average annual temperature of 26.025°.

What is the difference in temperature between these two cities? You can find out by subtracting the smaller number from the larger one:

$$76.975 - 26.025 = 50.95$$

So, between the average annual temperature for Honolulu and Fairbanks there is a difference of 50.95 degrees.

Note that the average annual temperature for Fairbanks, Alaska, is below freezing. How many degrees below freezing is it?

Again, you can find out by using subtraction. You may have noticed that the temperature for Fairbanks is a decimal number. To make the math easier, you can round off the number for the Fairbanks temperature to a whole number, which is a number without any decimal places.

Look at the Fairbanks number again:

$$26.025$$

Since the first number after the decimal place is zero, you can round this number down to just 26. This makes the math you need to do much simpler:

$$32 - 26 = 6$$

So, on average, the temperature in Fairbanks, Alaska, is about six degrees below freezing. Sounds like a pretty cold place!

◄ *In some parts of Alaska, the average temperature is rarely above freezing. This is what could be described as a cold climate.*

CLIMATE PART 2: PRECIPITATION

What's the nearest source of water to you at this very moment?

What was your answer? The kitchen sink? The pond in your backyard? The drinking fountain in the school hallway?

Well, those are all correct, but did you know that there is water in the air around you? This is the same water that condenses to form clouds, and it can make you feel uncomfortable on a hot and humid summer day.

There are also times when the air is loaded with so much water that it actually falls out of the sky. You are talking now about different types of precipitation, forms of water that fall to the earth's surface. The form of precipitation that most people are familiar with is rain.

Some parts of the United States, like Seattle, Washington, and Indianapolis, Indiana, are famous for receiving large amounts of rainfall. ▶

Rain is a big factor in determining the climate of an area. The amount of rain a place gets can determine if that area is a **desert** or a **rain forest**, or somewhere in between.

What images come to mind when you hear the term *desert?* Sand? Snakes? Maybe palm trees?

In fact, what makes a desert a desert is the amount of rainfall it receives. A desert is an area that receives no more than 10 inches of rainfall per year. And, although the temperatures in a desert are usually high during the day, they can get very cold at night.

There are even snowy deserts! The Arctic, for instance, might not look like the kind of desert you imagine in your mind, but because it receives less than 10 inches of rainfall in an average year, it is, by definition, a desert.

Meanwhile, you're probably also familiar with the term rain forest. A rain forest is pretty much what it sounds like: a thick forest that receives a great deal of rain. But how much rain? To qualify as a rain forest, an area must receive at least 100 inches of rainfall per year.

If the average annual rainfall for a rain forest is at least 100 inches, and the average annual rainfall for a desert is about 10 inches, how many more inches of rainfall does a rain forest receive compared to a desert?

You can find out by subtracting:

$$100 - 10 = 90$$

A rain forest receives about 90 more inches of rain every year than a desert!

There are four large deserts in the United States, all of them located in the Southwest. These include:

The Chihuahuan Desert

The Great Basin Desert

The Mojave Desert

The Sonoran Desert

You might also be surprised to find out that there are some rain forests in the United States! These include the Hoh Rain forest in Olympia, Washington, and the Kauai Rain forest, which is part of Hawaii.

Let's take a look at two charts based on data collected at weather observing stations in the United States. The first is a list of ten places that receive a great deal of rainfall:

#	Location	State	Inches
1	Mt. Washington	New Hampshire	89.92
2	Mobile	Alabama	64.64
3	New Orleans	Louisiana	59.74
4	Miami	Florida	57.55
5	Baton Rouge	Louisiana	55.77
6	Birmingham	Alabama	54.52
7	Juneau	Alaska	53.15
8	Jackson	Mississippi	52.82
9	Jacksonville	Florida	52.76
10	Charleston	South Carolina	51.59

*Source: Infoplease.com - Climate of 100 Selected U.S. Cities

The second chart lists spots that receive very little rainfall:

91	Tucson	Arizona	11.14
92	Fairbanks	Alaska	10.37
93	Roswell	New Mexico	9.7
94	San Diego	California	9.32
95	Albuquerque	New Mexico	8.12
96	Grand Junction	Colorado	8
97	El Paso	Texas	7.82
98	Reno	Nevada	7.49
99	Phoenix	Arizona	7.11
100	Las Vegas	Nevada	4.19

*Source: Infoplease.com - Climate of 100 Selected U.S. Cities

Notice anything? The bottom, or "driest" places are all located in the Southwest—in other words, they are all in the desert!

Now compare some of the information you have. Look at the two extremes—the "wettest" city and the "driest" locations. How many more inches of rain does Mt. Washington, New Hampshire, receive compared to Las Vegas, Nevada?

All you have to do is subtract the smaller number from the bigger number:

$89.92 - 4.19 = 85.73$

So in an average year, Mt. Washington, New Hampshire, receives about 86 more inches of rain than Las Vegas, Nevada!

The cactus is one of the few forms of plant life that can thrive in the desert. This is because of a large root system that allows the cactus to store water for long periods of time.

Dew

Strictly speaking, **dew** is not a form of precipitation. This is because precipitation involves *falling*. Both snow and rain, for instance, fall from the sky. Dew, on the other hand, merely *collects*.

Dew usually forms at night when the temperature of the air cools. When this happens, the ability of the air to retain moisture lessens. As the water vapor in the air condenses, it ends up on leaves, cars, grass, or just about any stationary object. If the air is unusually cold, the dew will freeze and become frost.

Have you ever gone outside on a cool morning and found dew? What does that tell you about the weather conditions of the night before?

SNOWFALL

Have you ever been looking forward to a snow day only to be disappointed when it rained instead of snowed? Snow is a tricky thing. In order for it to snow, the temperature has to be just right.

You probably never knew this, but most precipitation starts as snow. That is because high up, in the troposphere, it is always cold.

As you learned before, the freezing temperature for water is 32°. If the outside temperature is much warmer than that, the precipitation that leaves the clouds as snow melts on the way down to earth and hits the ground as rain.

Snow impairs visibility and makes driving dangerous. Heavy amounts of snowfall can even result in school being cancelled. However, very specific atmospheric conditions need to be met in order for snow to occur.

When snow does fall, though, it can be a fun, magical event. That is, until your parents ask you to do the shoveling!

Depending on where you live, though, you may never have even seen snow. Let's take a look at some more charts. This time, we'll be looking at the ten top and ten bottom locations for snowfall. First, the top ten:

#	Location	State	Inches
1	Mt. Washington	New Hampshire	246.8
2	Caribou	Maine	113.3
3	Juneau	Alaska	102.8
4	Buffalo	New York	92.2
5	Casper	Wyoming	80.5
6	Burlington	Vermont	78.2
7	Duluth	Minnesota	77.4
8	Portland	Maine	72.4
9	Grand Rapids	Michigan	72.4
10	Anchorage	Alaska	69.2

*Source: Infoplease.com - Climate of 100 Selected U.S. Cities

And now the bottom ten:

83	Houston	Texas	0.4
84	San Antonio	Texas	0.4
85	Mobile	Alabama	0.3
86	Savannah	Georgia	0.3
87	Montgomery	Alabama	0.3
88	New Orleans	Louisiana	0.2
89	Baton Rouge	Louisiana	0.1
90	Sacramento	California	0.1
91	Miami	Florida	0
92	Honolulu	Hawaii	0

*Source: Infoplease.com - Climate of 100 Selected U.S. Cities

It should be noted here that Florida has received traces of snow in the past, but not really enough to measure. Meanwhile, the fact that Honolulu, Hawaii never receives any snow probably isn't a surprise to you. Especially considering that you already learned the average temperature in Honolulu is 77°!

Honolulu, Hawaii, is most certainly a part of the United States. It is, however, an island in the Pacific Ocean. For comparison, let's instead use two places in the **continental** United States. How about Buffalo, New York, and Mobile, Alabama?:

Buffalo	92.2
Mobile	0.3

In an average year, how many more inches of snow does Buffalo, New York, receive than Mobile, Alabama?

$$92.2 - 0.3 = 91.9$$

So Buffalo, New York typically receives about 91.9 inches more snow in a year than Mobile, Alabama!

Just to put all that in perspective, maybe you should calculate how many feet of snow that is. Remember, there are 12 inches in a foot. In order to figure out how many feet 91.9 inches is, you'll need to divide 91.9 by 12:

$$91.9 \div 12 = 7.65$$

So Buffalo, New York, gets about seven more feet of snow in a year than Mobile, Alabama! That sounds like a lot of shoveling!

WIND

You've probably given a lot of thought to different wind conditions without even realizing it. If you want to fly a kite, for instance, you have to wait for a good breeze. You've probably also worn an item of clothing called a windbreaker, which is perfect for keeping warm on a windy spring day. But did you know that there is a scale for measuring wind?

Using the Beaufort scale as a reference, what would you say is a good strength of wind for kite flying? How would that strength compare to the speed of a strong gale?

The Beaufort Scale was developed in 1806 by Admiral Sir Francis Beaufort of the British navy. It is the most common method of measurement for wind speeds:

Force	Description	Wind speed (mph)	Conditions
0	Calm	0	Smoke rises vertically
1	Light air	1-3	Smoke drifts
2	Light breeze	4-7	Leaves rustle; vane moved by wind
3	Gentle breeze	8-12	Leaves in constant motion; light flag extended
4	Moderate breeze	13-18	Raises dust and loose paper; small branches move
5	Fresh breeze	19-24	Small trees sway; crested wavelets on inland water
6	Strong breeze	25-31	Large branches in motion
7	Moderate gale	32-38	Whole trees in motion
8	Fresh gale	39-46	Breaks twigs off trees; impedes walking
9	Strong gale	47-54	Slight structural damage to buildings
10	Whole gale	55-63	Large branches broken; some trees uprooted
11	Storm	64-72	Large trees uprooted
12	Hurricane	73+	Widespread damage occurs

*Source: Kites.org

As you can see, on the Beaufort Scale, winds are measured in terms of miles per hour. They are also categorized according to different strengths. The lightest wind, the one that travels at roughly 1-3 miles per hour, is a Force 1 wind. The next level up, a wind traveling at 4-7 miles per hour, is a Force 2 wind.

Using the Beaufort Scale, can you determine the difference in miles per hour between a moderate breeze and a strong gale?

This is a bit tricky, because with the Beaufort Scale you're not dealing with single numbers. Instead, you're dealing with a **series** of numbers.

Simply put, a series is a sequence of numbers. Take a look at the Beaufort Scale measurement for a moderate breeze:

Moderate breeze   13-18

What this means is that a moderate breeze is any wind traveling between 13 and 18 miles per hour.

In order to determine the difference in miles per hour between a moderate breeze and a strong gale, you need to find the **medians** of these series. The median is the middle number in a series of numbers.

Although they are not the same things, finding the median of a series of numbers is very much like calculating an average. It is a two-step process involving addition, followed by division.

First of all, find the median for a moderate breeze. To start, you add the numbers of the series:

$$13 + 14 + 15 + 16 + 17 + 18 = 93$$

Then, you divide the result by the number of addends:

$$93 \div 6 = 15.5$$

So, the median for a moderate breeze is 15.5!

Now let's calculate the median for a strong gale. If you refer to the Beaufort Scale, you can see that a strong gale is:

Strong gale   47-54

So, add the numbers in the series:

$$47 + 48 + 49 + 50 + 51 + 52 + 53 + 54 = 404$$

Then divide the result by the number of addends:

$$404 \div 8 = 50.5$$

Now you know that the median for a strong gale is 50.5, and the median for a moderate breeze is 15.5. All you have to do now to calculate the difference is to subtract the smaller number from the larger number:

$$50.5 - 15.5 = 35$$

The difference between a strong gale and a moderate breeze is about 35 miles per hour!

HURRICANES AND TORNADOES

Just as water and precipitation play a big part in determining the climate of a particular area, wind plays a key role in providing storms with their power. The stronger the wind, the more powerful the storm, and, for good reason, the more frightening it can be.

To qualify as a hurricane, a storm's winds have to be traveling at speeds of 73 miles per hour or greater.

Perhaps you noticed in the last section that the Beaufort Scale ends at 73+ miles per hour. This is because winds stronger than 73 miles per hour indicate a **hurricane**. A hurricane is a type of storm that forms over the ocean and occasionally travels over land. If you have ever seen a satellite photo of a hurricane, you know that the winds of a hurricane travel in a swirling, circular pattern like water going down a drain.

Hurricane winds have their own scale of measurement: the Saffir-Simpson Scale. The category, or force of a hurricane, is used to estimate the potential damage a hurricane might cause:

Category	Wind Speed
1	74 to 95 mph
2	96 to 110 mph
3	111 to 130 mph
4	131 to 155 mph
5	Greater than 155 mph

*Source: Homepage of the National Oceanic and Atmospheric Administration

How much more powerful are the winds of a category 4 hurricane compared to a category 2 hurricane?

As with the winds on the Beaufort Scale, you're dealing with series. Because the winds of a hurricane are so powerful, though, you're dealing with much larger numbers.

Take a look at the range for a category 4 hurricane:

131 – 155 mph

It would take a while for you to add up every single number between 131 and 155. Instead, you're going to use a short cut. You're going to add up just the two *end* numbers, and then divide by two:

$$131 + 155 = 286$$
$$286 \div 2 = 143$$

Therefore, the winds of a category 4 hurricane are roughly 143 miles per hour.

Now perform the same calculations for the winds of a category 2 hurricane:

$$96 + 110 = 206$$
$$206 \div 2 = 103$$

Therefore, the winds of a category 2 hurricane are about 103 miles per hour.

So, to answer the original question—how much more powerful are the winds of a category 4 hurricane compared to a category two hurricane—you just need to subtract.

$$143 - 103 = 40$$

The winds of a category 4 hurricane are about 40 miles per hour stronger than the winds of a category 2 hurricane. You can see how winds that powerful could cause a lot of damage. You wouldn't even be able to stand up in winds that strong!

Tornadoes are another kind of windstorm. Like hurricanes, the winds of a tornado travel in a circular pattern. The winds of a tornado, however, are tighter and more concentrated. That is why a hurricane cannot really be seen on land, while tornadoes are clearly visible as twisting, dancing "funnels."

Just as hurricanes have a scale of measurement, tornadoes are measured according to the Fujita Scale:

Level	Wind Speed
F0	40-72 mph
F1	73-112 mph
F2	113-157 mph
F3	158-206 mph
F4	207-260 mph
F5	261-318 mph

*Source: National Hurricane Center

Using the Fujita scale, how much faster are the winds of a force 5 tornado compared to the winds of a force 1 tornado?

You can use the same shortcut you employed earlier for determining the medians of these numbers:

Level 1: $73 + 112 = 185 \div 2 = 92.5$

Level 5: $261 + 318 = 579 \div 2 = 289.5$

Now all you have to do is subtract:

$289.5 - 92.5 = 197$

The winds of a force 5 tornado are about 197 miles per hour stronger than the winds of a force 1 tornado!

Blizzards

Have you ever lived through a blizzard? In many ways, a blizzard is something of a combination between a typical snowstorm and the kind of high-speed winds usually associated with a hurricane.

Actually, the winds of a blizzard are significantly lower than that of a typical hurricane. In order to qualify as a blizzard, the winds of a storm must be traveling at speeds greater than 35 mph. How much slower is that than the winds of a hurricane?

You can find out by subtracting:

$74 - 35 = 39$

The winds of a blizzard are roughly 39 mph slower than those of a hurricane!

CONCLUSION

Now that you have read this book, you know that math isn't just numbers on a piece of paper. It is a tool that you can use to understand the world you live in.

The importance of math becomes especially clear when you consider the cases where weather math has helped people—and even saved lives.

Think about it. Math is how meteorologists know to tell us if we should bring an umbrella when we leave the house. It is how they know to tell us if we should avoid too much physical activity in dangerously hot weather.

If you have enjoyed learning how to use math to understand the weather, maybe you will want to learn more about meteorology.

Maybe you'll even want to consider becoming a meteorologist yourself!

◀ *Blizzards are snowstorms with high-speed winds. The winds of a blizzard, however, are not nearly as fast as those of a hurricane.*

THE METRIC SYSTEM

We actually have two systems of weights and measure in the United States. Quarts, pints, gallons, ounces, and pounds are all units of the U.S. Customary System, also known as the English System.

The other system of measurement, and the only one sanctioned by the United States Government, is the metric system, which is also known as the International System of Units. French scientists developed the metric system in the 1790s.

There are a number of ways that the metric system applies to weather. First of all, when measuring temperature, most of the world does not use the Fahrenheit system. Instead, they rely on the Celsius Scale, which treats the freezing point of water as 0° and the boiling point as 100°.

Converting a Fahrenheit reading to a Celsius reading is quite simple. Just subtract 32 from the Fahrenheit temperature and then divide the result by 1.8.

For instance, room temperature is about 72°. What is that on the Celsius scale?

$$72 - 32 = 40$$
$$40 \div 1.8 = 22.2$$

Room temperature is about 22° Celsius!

Another instance where you may need to apply metric measurements to weather concepts is with precipitation. Rainfall and snowfall, for example, are measured in the United States by inches, but these readings would be done in centimeters for most of the world. A centimeter is roughly equal to 0.39 of an inch—a little less than half an inch. There are 2.56 cm to an inch.

So, if Mt. Washington, New Hampshire receives 89.92 inches of rain in a typical year, how many centimeters of rain is that? You can find out by using multiplication:

$$89.92 \times 2.56 = 230$$

230 centimeters!

Finally, you know that wind measurements in the United States are typically expressed in miles per hour. In the metric system, though, these would be in kilometers per hour (kph). One mile is equal to about 1.6 kilometers. Therefore, if you know a hurricane's winds are traveling at 85 mph, how fast are they traveling in kph?

$$85 \times 1.6 = 136$$

136 kilometers per hour!

As you can see, the metric system is pretty easy once you get the hang of it. For practice, you could go through this book and convert some of the numbers to metric. Try it!

GLOSSARY

addends – the numbers added together in an addition problem

altitude – height

atmosphere – a layer of gases that surrounds a planet

climate – the type of weather usually experienced in a particular place over a long period of time

condenses – turns from gas to liquid

continental – part of a large land mass

desert – an area that receives no more than 10 inches of rainfall per year

dew – A form of moisture that collects, rather than falls, on surfaces. Usually caused by cooling temperatures at night

hurricane – a kind of storm typified by swirling winds of more than 73 miles per hour

medians – the middle number in a series of numbers

mercury – a silver substance that is liquid at room temperature

meteorologist – a scientist who studies the behavior of a planet's atmosphere

precipitation – a form of water that falls to the earth's surface

rain forest – an area that receives at least 100 inches of rainfall per year

series – one of a group

tornadoes – storms typified by swirling winds of more than 40 miles per hour

troposphere – the lowest layer of gases in the earth's atmosphere

vapor – the gaseous form of a substance

Further Reading

O'Hare, Ted. *Weather Report: Clouds.*
Rourke Publishing, LLC., 2003.

O'Hare, Ted. *Weather Report: Rain, Snow, and Ice.*
Rourke Publishing, LLC., 2003.

O'Hare, Ted. *Weather Report: Storms.*
Rourke Publishing, LLC., 2003.

O'Hare, Ted. *Weather Report: Studying Weather.*
Rourke Publishing, LLC., 2003.

O'Hare, Ted. *Weather Report: The Weather and Us.*
Rourke Publishing, LLC., 2003.

O'Hare, Ted. *Weather Report: Weather Signs.*
Rourke Publishing, LLC., 2003.

Zeman, Anne and Kate Kelly. *Everything You Need To Know About Math Homework*. Scholastic, 1994.

Websites to Visit

http://science.howstuffworks.com/hurricane.htm
How Stuff Works – How Hurricanes Work

http://www.kites.org/jo/beaufort.html
Kites.org – The Beaufort Scale

http://www.tornadoproject.com/fscale/fscale.htm
The Fujita Scale of Tornado Intensity

INDEX

altitude   8

atmosphere   6, 7

average annual temperatures
    15, 18, 19

Beaufort Scale   34, 35, 36, 38

blizzards   41

climate   15, 24

clouds   7, 8, 9, 22

    cirrus   7, 8, 9

    cumulus   7

    stratus   7, 8, 9

desert   24, 25, 27

dew   28

Fahrenheit, Gabriel Daniel   14

frost   28

Fujita Scale   40

hurricanes   38, 39, 40, 41, 45

mercury thermometer   14

meteorologist   4, 6, 43

metric system   44

precipitation   15, 22, 28, 45

rain   4, 6, 22, 24, 25, 26, 27, 29, 45

rain forest   24, 25

room temperature   12

Saffir-Simpson Scale   38

snow   4, 29, 30, 31, 41, 45

storm   4, 6, 37

temperature   4, 6, 10, 11, 12, 14,
    15, 16, 18, 21, 24, 28, 31

tornadoes   40, 41

troposphere   6, 7

U. S. Customary System   44

vapor   7, 28

wind   32, 34, 37, 38, 39, 40, 41, 45

About The Author

Kieran Walsh has written a variety of children's nonfiction books, primarily on historical and social studies topics, including the recent Rourke series *Holiday Celebrations* and *Countries in the News.* He divides his time between upstate New York and New York City.